Quotes for Personal Excellence – 5

Moods and Emotions

One Hundred Quotes and Thoughts with One Hundred Insightful Illustrations of Lord Ganesha

R.N. Kogata • Lalita Kogata

DK PRINTWORLD
Publishers of Indian Traditions

First Published in India, 2014
ISBN 13: 978-81-246-0673-5
ISBN 10: 81-246-0673-0

A creation of:
Mr R.N. Kogata and Mrs Lalita Kogata
608, Hiran Magari, Sector - 11, Udaipur, India
Phones: +91-94141 58870, +91-294-258 3870
devkush@rediffmail.com

Printed and published by:
D.K. Printworld (P) Ltd.
'Vedasri', F-395, Sudarshan Park
(Metro Station: Ramesh Nagar), New Delhi - 110 015
Phones: 011-2545 3975 / 2546 6019 Fax: 011-2546 5926
e-mail: indology@dkprintworld.com Web: www.dkprintworld.com

Preface

Mood is a basic psychological state that can occur as a reaction to an event or can surface for no apparent external cause. Mood is an internal, subjective state, but it often can be inferred from posture, facial expression and other behaviours. Mood can also be described as a mental state or quality of feeling at a particular time, a prevailing emotional surge or general attitude, a frame of mind evasive or receptive.

Mood generally is indicative of a positive or negative state of mind. Positive mood can be attributed to many different aspects of day-to-day life and has certain effects on people as a whole. Generally, positive mood has been found enhancing problem-solving ability and general flexibility. Like positive mood, negative mood also does have important implications for mental and physical well-being. Since there is no intentional objective that causes the negative mood, it has no specific time-frame. Negative moods can manipulate the way individuals interpret and translate the world around them, and can also direct their behaviour.

Emotion is a complex psycho-physiological experience of an individual's state of mind caused by interacting with biochemical (internal) and environmental (external) influences. Emotion is associated with mood, temperament, personality, disposition and motivation. Motivations direct and energize behaviour, while emotions provide the effective component to motivation, positive or negative. All humans have basic emotional needs. These needs can be expressed as feelings. The only real way to know that we are happy is when we feel happy. When we feel happy, we feel contented and fulfilled. This feeling comes from having our needs and desires met, particularly our emotional needs. We can be warm, wealthy and healthy, but still unhappy. Our emotions and our feelings let us know when we are unhappy and when something vital is missing or needed. The better we understand our emotions, the easier to determine what is really needed to be happy.

Our emotions put us alert on when natural human needs are not being met or when we feel uncomfortable for any reason. While all humans share almost the same needs, each individual differs in the intensity of the need.

Our emotions are a valuable source of information and help us to communicate and make decisions. Our feelings are also useful in helping us predict our own and others' behaviour. Emotions are universal.

This book contains 100 carefully chosen quotations on Moods and Emotions, created, modified and mixed. Some of the thoughts presented here are ours and the others are from the people who have stood by and worked for the values, some were famous and others were ordinary people. We have acknowledged the persons who have been quoted, wherever we could remember. Our sincere thanks to all these great personalities and eminent writers who have given such invaluable thoughts to this world. Any amendment/addition is most welcome from the readers.

Ganesha gives peace, prosperity and wisdom and, therefore, each of the quotes in this book has a painting of Lord Ganesha to inspire you. These paintings have been created by our professional artists keeping in mind the themes of individual quotes.

Inspiring ourselves with the fact that good thoughts can lead to changes in our habits, attitude and behaviour, and can help us improve our outlook of the world and thus change our lives, we have conceived the idea of this book. This kind of a book is like chewing each morsel well, while enjoying the good food and then digesting it before getting ready for the next meal.

We prostrate before our parents Smt Kanchan Devi and Shri Bhairav Lal Kogata, and Smt Kamla Devi Nuwal and the late Prof. K.M. Nuwal for their benign blessings that have helped us reach the present stage.

With the expectation of blessings and constructive feedback from all our readers.

Lalita & R.N. Kogata

Acknowledgement

Quotations from some eminent writers, philosophers and great personalities have been included in this book. Details of the same are given below. We sincerely thank all of them.

Page No.	Quotation by	Page No.	Quotation by	Page No.	Quotation by
7	George Eliot	41	William Arthur Ward	76	Mahatma Gandhi
8	Plato	42	Eric Hoffe	77	Howard Mumford Jones
10	Louisa May Alcott	43	Don Williams, Jr.	79	F. Scott Fitzgerald
14	Francis Bacon	45	Dale Carnegie	80	Khalil Gibran
15	Earl Nightingale	46	Max Eastman and Mary Hirsch	81	Douglas H. Everett
16	Russell H. Ewing	47	Benjamin Franklin	82	Donald Curtis
17	St Catherin of Siena	49	Bliss Carma	85	Dorothy Canfield Fisher
18	James Cameron	50	Martin Fraquhar Tupper	86	Oscar Wilde
19	Havelock Ellis	51	Oscar Wilde	87	Jim Rohn
20	John Balguy	54	Drew Carey	88	Margaret Thatcher
21	Christian Bovee	55	Jesse Jackson	89	Mignon McLaughlin
22	Steve Jobs	56	Dennis Prager	90	John Wooden
25	Colette	57	Arnold Glasow	91	Saint Laurent
26	Judith Guest	58	Jules Renard	92	Arthur Ashe
27	Gail Devers	59	Confucius and Albert Einstein	93	William James
29	Konstantin Stanislavsky	60	Orson Welles	94	Ronald Reagan
30	Johann Wolfgang	63	Robert Francis Kennedy	95	John Lubbock
31	Ralph Waldo Emerson	64	Pearl S. Buck	96	Oscar Wilde
32	Antonio Porchia	65	George Foreman	97	Soren Kierkegaard
33	Norman Vincent Peale	66	Bertrand Russell	98	Robert H. Schuller
34	Cullen Hightower	67	Drew Deyoung	99	Aristotle
35	E.W. Howe	68	John Maxwell	100	Benjamin Franklin
36	Bob Marley	70	Mother Teresa	102	Oscar Wilde
37	William Penn	71	Antoine de Saint	104	Epictetus
39	Oscar Wilde	73	Alan Lakein	105	Francis Bacon, Sr.
40	Sophia Loren	75	Samuel Johnson		

Adventure is not an external feature;

it is within.

We can easily forgive
a child who is afraid of darkness;

the real tragedy of life is
when one gets afraid of light.

Aggressive

Stay calm and aggressive,

but aggression should not kill
your romantic quality.

Ambitious

Far away there in the sunshine
are my highest aspirations.

I may not reach them,
but I can look up
and see their beauty,
believe in them
and try to follow them.

If you are right
then there is no need to get angry,

and

if you are wrong,
then you don't have any right
to get angry.

Anxiety is the rust in life,
destroying its brightness and
weakening its strength.

A childlike and abiding trust
in providence
is its best prevention and remedy.

Apologizing doesn't mean
you are right or wrong,

it just means
you value your relationship
more than your ego.

Bashful

Bashfulness is a great hindrance to a man;
both in uttering his sentiments and
in understanding what is proposed to him.

It is, therefore, good
to press forward with discretion,
both in discourse and company
of the better sort.

You will feel boredom
when you experience
the absence of a good idea.

A boss creates fear, a leader instils confidence.
A boss fixes blame, a leader corrects mistakes.
A boss drives, a leader leads.
A boss knows all, a leader asks questions.
A boss makes work drudgery, a leader makes it interesting.

To a brave man,
good and bad luck
are like right and left hands.

He uses both.

There are many talented people
who haven't fulfilled their dreams,
because they overthought it,
or they were too cautious,
and were unwilling to
take the leap of faith.

Charm means
the power to execute work
without employing brute force
and is indispensable to women.

Charm is a woman's strength
as strength is a man's charm.

Complacence is an invaluable pearl,
and whoever procures it
may be at any cost
makes a wise and happy purchase.

Confident

Whatever might be their strength,
they are the weakest,
who have no confidence in themselves
or in their powers.

Creativity and innovation
distinguish one
between a leader and a follower.

Cultivate curiosity,

for it is the seedbed of discovery
and the author of invention.

Defensive

Love is much like a wild rose,
beautiful and calm,

but willing to draw
blood in its defence.

I am delighted,
what a wonderful life
I have had!

I only wish
I had realized it long back!

Depression is not sobbing,
crying and giving vent to feelings.
It is plain and simple
reduction of feelings . . .

People who keep stiff upper lip
find damn hard to smile.

Keep your dreams alive.
Understand that to achieve anything
requires faith and belief in yourself,
vision, hardwork, determination and dedication.

Remember, all things are possible only for
those who believe in themselves!

Disappointment to a noble soul
is what cold water is
to the burning metal;

it strengthens, intensifies, tempers,
but never destroys the metal.

The language of the body,
however dramatic, is the key
that can unlock the soul.

What is uttered earnestly
from the heart alone
will win the hearts
of others to your own.

Can anything be as elegant
as to have few wants
and to serve them oneself?

Elevated

If you don't raise your eyes,
you will think you are at the peak point.

The more you lose yourself in something bigger than you, the more will be your energy and excitement.

People seldom become famous
for what they say
until they are famous
for what they have done.

To avoid mistakes and regrets,
always consult your wife
before engaging in flirtation.

When you dream of a bright future,
you can't forget the past.

A true friend
speaks freely,
advises justly,
assists readily,
adventures boldly,
takes all patiently,
defends courageously, and
continues to be a friend
unchangeably.

Forget your enemies.

It is your friends you frustrate
who cause you all the problems.

A gentleman is one
who never hurts anyone's feelings
unintentionally.

Ha . . . Ha . . . Ha . . .

Beauty and true glamour
are mere inner feelings;
they reflect in your eyes.

And, they aren't something
physical.

Grateful

Feeling gratitude and not
expressing it
is like wrapping a present
and not giving it away.

Harshness is
the weak man's
imitation of strength.

God talks incessantly.

But, as it turns out,
mankind is deaf.

It is better
to deserve honour
and not to have it

than to have it
when not deserving it.

Hostile

Fear not those
who are hostile
and argue

but those
who dodge.

Humour is the
instinct for taking
pain playfully.

It is a rubber sword –
it allows you to
make a point
without drawing blood.

The greatest ignorance is
to reject something you know
nothing about,

and

being ignorant is
not so much a shame,
as being unwilling to learn.

If we are going
in the right direction,
all we have to do is
keep on walking,
and don't get impatient.

Indifference may not wreck
a man's life at any one turn,

but it will destroy him
with a kind of dry-rot
in the long run.

A baby in the house is
a well-spring of pleasure,
a messenger of peace and love,
a resting place for innocence on earth,
a link between angels and men.

Insecure

There are many things
that we would throw away

if we weren't afraid
that others might pick them up.

I know that I am bright
because I know about
how much I know,

and

I know that I am intelligent,
because I make mistakes,
but quickly correct them.

Jealous

The jealous are
troublesome for others,
but a torment to themselves,

and they are always
born with love,
but always die without it.

Oh, you hate your job?
Why didn't you say so?

There's a support group for that.
It's called EVERYBODY,
and they meet at the bar, jubilantly.

Never look down on anybody
unless you're helping him up.

One of the perilous mind destroyers
of students is the belief that
if it's very complex or knotty,
it's very profound,
thoughtful and intense.

Laughter
is a tranquillizer
with no side effects.

Laziness is nothing more
than the habit of resting
before you get really tired.

Real literacy and knowledge are to know
the extent of one's ignorance,
but imagination is more important
than literacy and knowledge,
which are limited, . . .

. . . It encircles the whole world.

We are born alone,
we live alone,
and die alone.

Only through love and friendship
we can create the illusion
for the moment that
we aren't alone.

The loveliest and the greatest treasures are those that are invisible to the eye but found by the heart.

Say what you mean,
mean what you say,

but don't ever
say it "mean".

What is objectionable,
what is dangerous,
what is mischievous
about extremists is not that
they are extreme,
but that they are intolerant.

The evil is not what
they say about their cause,
but what they say
about their opponents.

I don't wait for moods.
You accomplish nothing
if you do that.

Your mind must know
it has to get down to work.

That is my gift.
I let that negativity
roll off me
like water off a duck's back.

If it's not positive,
I don't hear it.

If you follow this policy,
fights become easy.

Nervous

One of the symptoms of
an approaching
nervous breakdown
is the belief that
one's work
is terribly important.

Of course,
I look at the glass that is
half full.

The only time I would look at
it's empty half is
when I think about
how good
the first half tasted.

A great leader's courage
to fulfil his vision
comes from passion,

not from position.

Patience with family is love,
Patience with others is respect,
Patience with self is confidence,
and
Patience with GOD is faith.

If we have no peace,
it is because
we have forgotten that
we belong to each other.

Perfection is achieved,

not when there is
nothing more to add,

but when there is
nothing left to take away.

One who feels bad when he feels good
for the fear that he'll feel worse
when he feels better.

Somebody, who complains
about the noise when opportunity knocks,
finds excuse for not trying,
guarantees himself a failure.

Planning is bringing
the future into the present,
so that you can do
something about it now.

He, who allows his day to pass by
without practising generosity
and enjoying life's pleasures,
is like a blacksmith's bellows:

It breathes but doesn't live.

Politeness is one of
those qualities
which we never
estimate rightly but
by the inconvenience
caused with its loss.

Positive

Keep your thoughts positive because
they become your words.

Keep your words positive because
they become your deeds.

Keep your deeds positive because
they become your habits.

Keep your habits positive because
they become your lifestyle.

Keep your lifestyle positive because
it becomes your fortune.

This is the era,
in which
we are proud of machines
that think, and suspicious of men
who try to reconstruct.

Do not be afraid of failure.
Don't waste energy trying to cover up failure.
Learn from the mistakes that led you to failures.

Provoke yourself to go on to the next challenge,
accept it so that you may one day
feel the exhilaration of victory.

It is OK to fail.
If you aren't failing,
you aren't growing.

Family quarrels are bitter things.
They don't go according to rules.
They aren't like routine aches or wounds.

They are more like splits in the skin
that won't heal, because there isn't
enough material left to seal them.

If we all confess
our sins to one another,
we would all laugh at
one another for our lack
of individual originality.

There are some people,
who live in a dreamworld
and there are some
who face the reality.

Then there are those
who turn one into the other.

Relaxation means releasing
all concerns and tensions and
letting the natural order of life
flow through one's being.

There is no feeling more relieving, comforting and consoling than knowing that you are sitting right next to the one you love.

Working positively is much
more important than being a star.

You should not only be very
famous or respected right now,
but should also be respected,
loved, remembered and understood
for a hundred years after your death.

It is not good for all our wishes to be fulfilled.
Through sickness we realize the value of health;
through evil, the value of good;
through hunger, the value of food;
through exertion, the value of rest;
through restlessness, the value of peace.

To love one's self is the
beginning of a lifelong romance.

The walls
that we build around us
to keep discomfort
and sadness out,

also keep the joy out.

Satisfied

Look at a day when you are
well satisfied at the end.

It isn't a day when you
lounged around doing nothing;
it is when you've had a lot to do,
and you've done it!

Self-conscious

Once you become self-conscious,
there is no end to it.

Once you start to doubt,
there is no room left for anything else.

Consider the rights of others
before your own feelings and sentiments,

and

the feelings and sentiments of others
before your own rights.

Fashions fade,
but style and smartness
are eternal
and evergreen.

You have got to get to the
stage in life where going for it
is more important
than winning or losing.

Live a sparkling life!

The greatest weapon
against stress
is our own ability
to choose one thought
over the other.

Surround yourself
with the best people
you can find,

delegate authority,
be strict
and don't interfere.

Do not be afraid of showing your affection.

Be warm and tender,
thoughtful and affectionate.

Men are more helped
by sympathy, than by service.

Love is more than money,
and a kind word
will give more pleasure
than a present.

I am the only person in the world,

I should like to know everything thoroughly.

People demand freedom of
speech as a compensation
for the freedom of thought,
which they seldom use.

As we grow as unique persons,
we must learn to respect the
uniqueness of others.

Suffering becomes beautiful
when we bear great calamities
and victimization with cheerfulness,
and fortitude,

not through insensibility,
but through greatness of mind.

When you are victorious, you must not
use any triumphing or insulting expression
nor show off too much of happiness,

but endeavour to console your adversary,
and make him less dissatisfied with himself
by every kind and civil expression.

Volatile

Irritability is immaturity of character.
If you are subject to being cross and
unpleasant with others for no apparent reason,
you need to come face-to-face with the fact
that you are thinking too much of yourself.

After all, your feelings aren't
the most important things in this world.

I have the simplest tastes.

I am always satisfied with the best.

If you are worthy,
you will get the
highest prize
by getting responsibility.

Do not seek to have
festivals and events happen
as you want them to,
but instead want them to
happen as they do happen,
enjoy them
and your life will go well.

Yearn

The yearning for power in excess
caused angels to fall;

the yearning for knowledge in excess
caused man to fall;

but in charity there is no excess,
neither man nor angels
come into danger by it.

Zig-Zaggy

Oh God!
You are all over the place!
Pranam!